"THE UBER CRAZE"

How to Make Money with Uber

Written by R.L. Smith

<u>**Dedication**</u>

I'm dedicating this book to all my fans and friends that love my work and supported me throughout the years. For those that are very interested in wanting to work from themselves and earn some incredible money working from home, this book is for you. I hope this book helps you in a very big way and serves as a guide to help you achieve your dreams. I'm looking forward to meeting you guys very soon.

Much Love,

R.L. Smith

TABLE OF CONTENT

Chapter 1:
Welcome to the World of Ridesharing

The World of Transportation Services Is Changing

The world of transportation is constantly changing, with new trends being introduced on a daily basis. The systems of transportation which our world has been built on are significantly changing. Intelligent transportation systems (ITS) are now leading to driving and traffic management becoming a lot better, effective, and safer. Also, soft infrastructure – the sphere of concepts, rules, and regulations- is constantly evolving to accommodate the increasing demand for international investment in transportation infrastructure. Nowadays, technology is successfully bridging the two of them as vehicles and infrastructure on which they work become increasingly connected. Traffic and the continuous growth of population create demand for transportation infrastructure. However, a lot of jurisdictions don't have enough money and space to build enough roads for everyone. Despite cities not having enough funds to support this, the fact is that populations will continue growing where the WHO expects 8 out of 10 people to be living in big cities by mid-century. Along with climate change worries, leaders must begin rethinking the nature of transportation systems and this is actually what is taking place. New transportation programs and technologies are constantly emerging to fulfill these challenges, along with connected vehicles, different types of fuels, fleet management, and analyzing traffic. New technology for high quality communications will change the way vehicles operate and offer information and systems for better traffic management. This is apparent with the introduction of Uber, which has become one of the most successful transportation companies in the world.

Before There Was Ridesharing...It Was Carpooling

Ride-sharing services were created from the desire to have a better and more effective option to taxis. In areas like San Francisco, where many top services are launched, cabs are hard to hail. Services such as Uber completely eliminated that. These days, the term ride-sharing can be somewhat of a misnomer, meaning that you're sharing a car or ride with someone in a carpool situation, where you arrive at a certain destination together. However, the fact is that the days of carpooling are completely gone now. Uber can be described as services that offer ride hailing, where you can easily request a ride from your mobile and then pay drivers for their services. There are many drivers who have been able to create a full business out of this actually.

The Death of the Taxi Industry

The days of standing on street corners and putting your hand out to grab the attention of a cab are completely gone. For city dwellers, hitching rides is now as simple as taking out your mobile, using the application, and then waiting for a well-trained driver to come take you. Look around major cities, and you're going to find that ride sharing services such as Uber are ubiquitous like taxis, if not completely overshadowing them. These services have clearly established themselves in cities such as New York, LA, and all over the world. It has become difficult to find a major city that Uber doesn't operate in.

Chapter 2:
The Rise of a New Phenomenon UBER

The New Phenomenon of the 21st Century
UBER

Created in 2009 by entrepreneurs Travis Kalanick and Garret Camp, Uber is a worldwide transportation network company which connects passengers with well-trained drives and ridesharing services using a mobile application. The Uber application connected riders with the divers using GPS capabilities, letting parties be aware of each other's location and eliminating the question of if the ride is going to arrive or not. Also, the technological company is responsible for processing all types of payments including charging the credit card of passengers, taking commissions (five to twenty percent) and depositing the money into the account of the driver. Based on availability, the company provided various service levels. The lowest price choice, UberX, runs in daily cars such as Toyota Prius. On the other hand, Uber black is the original price of the company, which costs more but passengers will be driven around in high end cars with professional drivers. UnberSux is exactly what it's like, charging a specific premium for a vehicle that is larger. Finally, Uber Lux is the final choice, operating in rides such as Porsches and BMW 7 sedans.

Guide to Uber Drivers

One of the main things that make Uber special is its drivers. Ubers requires that all its drivers pass both a DMV and background check. They should also have a car and it should be insured. Due to these minimal requirements, the service definitely attracts an array of individuals who are looking to make money and provide an efficient service at the time. For example, you can be picked one day by a biomedical engineer who works for Uber whereas another day you can be picked up by a doctor who is going this part time. Also, the company has introduced an Uber taxi service, which has been tested in different cities, and is used by taxis (based on local regulations). However, due to the fact that Uber X boasts rates that are 26% lower than cabs, you can imagine that it isn't necessarily a fixture you're going to find next to your cab meter.

Countries Where Uber Operates

In 45 countries and cities from Abu Dhabi to Zurich, the company's reach is staggering and its effect is unifying. If you know how to hail an Uber in Akron, Ohio you can also figure it out in TaiPei, Taiwan. Still, in the U.S., where regulations vary by city, county, and state, the service hasn't been allowed everywhere. For example, though it is legal to sleep on the sidewalk in Portland, Ore., you cannot hail an Uber there.

When Does Uber Actually Run?

Uber fancies itself more as a platform and less as an employer, so that's really a question for the drivers—and essentially, it's an issue of demand. In a 24-hour-per-day city like New York, there's always someone looking for a ride. But in smaller Uber bergs like Blacksburg, Virginia, the app is likely a dead zone in the middle of the night. Still, if you fire up the app and can see a car on the map, there's one nearby. Hail the ride and you'll get a fairly accurate estimated time of arrival. This Uber feature is a major draw, and compared to calling a taxi dispatcher and being given a rough estimate for arrival, there's no surprise why the service is doing so well.

Why Is Uber So Popular?

There is definitely more to Uber than a catchy and interesting name. The company has been able to capture its market share through a high quality app, remarkable social media marketing, and effectively courting drivers. The associated background technology is outstanding as well, connecting riders with drivers in a smooth interface that barely has any errors. The interface has more potential that only offering rides as well – in bringing ice cream, kittens, and even being a delivery service.

The Cost of Uber

That's definitely the most important question right? The answer is usually less. However, the math can be somewhat difficult to explain. Every ride has a specific base fair, and then a per-minute and mile charge is going to be added to it. Just like ordinary taxis, every city will have a completely different price. Fare estimates will be quoted early through the application. However, additional charges such as tolls or cleaning fees (if unfortunate accidents take place) will be added.

Also, based on supply and demand, the pricing of uber is subject to what is known as ''surge'' pricing, which increases rates considerably. Based on Uber's website the company currently utilizes this tactic to encourage drivers to become even more active during busy times.

What Makes Uber This Successful?

The growth and progress of Uber since 2009 has been unprecedented. During the previous twenty months alone, the amount of employees in the company grew from 700 employees to 5,000 from 66 cities to almost 341. Unfortunately, the company's net worth is almost $50 billion. However, this growth has been without any obstacles where the company continuous faces competition in every city it is in. The key to success here is that company was able to overcome every single one of these issues, and it is mainly related to the employees in the company.

Ownership is Key, Not Renting

Uber doesn't want employees working for the company to consider their job as a place where they spend a certain amount of hours and then collect pay checks. They want individuals to work for the company who legitimately care about the company. These are individuals who are going to act like company ''owners'' not individuals who are simply ''renting'' there. This is the main reason why the company has ''launchers''. These are individuals who are sent into places where the company expands into them. Their main job is recruiting the best drivers as possible, along with effectively building a team.

Take Bold Bets

The foundation of Uber was a bold bet that paid off. However, it didn't stop there, as employees working for the company continuously make bold bets so that company moves forward, with many of them even opening their own business. For example, Uber headquarters in Paris required more drivers so they sent a video out to 1 million French individuals who took Ubers previously. The move really worked, with thousands of individuals signing up so they become drivers after they saw the funny ad.

The Best Concept Wins....

Along the exact lines of taking bold bets, Uber emphasizes the concept, over individuals. The company attempts to ''prevent politics'' and support ''encourage toe stepping'' by continuously encouraging employees at different levels to voice new concepts. For example, in Chicago, recruits conducted interviews in an actual Uber ride instead of ordinary bureaucratic meetings. This actually resulted in more interesting prospects joining the company.

Chapter 3:
Starting Your Own Transportation Business With Uber

Why Starting A Business Now Is A Great Idea?

Although the dream of having their own business and being their own boss is classified under the 'may never happen' category of dreams, everything around is pointing towards a simple truth: now may be the best of times to abandon the old model and go into owning a business. Why? Read on, and you'll find out, and you may be surprised!

For one, the peak of the digital era is allowing for anyone to start, promote and run their small business while without having to hire experts and rely on other people in order to succeed. The vast array of apps, software and websites makes it easy to become a pro at previously complicated fields such as marketing, advertising, accounting, and the like.

Apart from apps, potential and current small business owners have at their disposal "the internet of things" which allows them to have access to any and all information pertaining to starting, running and expanding their business. From experts' blogs, through podcasts, all the way to online courses and webinars, individuals can expand their knowledge and get hands-on experience at a fraction of the cost of conventional education.

Moreover, today's economic environment is more than stimulating. With the worldwide economy recovering from recession, the prospect of getting credit from banks is becoming more and more viable with each day. Not only that, but consumer expenditure is following the trend, thus leaving plenty of space for service-oriented businesses to fill the void and expand.

Even more importantly, the global economy is rapidly moving towards what is known as "on-demand" working, with companies like Uber and AirBnB overcoming taxis and hotels in net worth and revenue with astounding speed. Therefore, it appears that there is no better time to adopt the model introduced by these companies, and reap the many benefits that come with abandoning the corporate world for the world of small business.

Finally, the idea of owning a business has always had, and continues to have, an appeal that can't be matched by working as an employee: the flexibility of working hours and ownership of earnings. As an employee, one is limited to working at a designated time for a set amount of money, while as a business owner (or partner) one has the opportunity to schedule their days in a way they find most suitable, and take responsibility of how much money they are going to make. In a nutshell, business owners can choose when they work, how much they work, and how much they charge for their services.

Have Vision of Your Life

The prospect of taking ownership of your time, work and earnings is closely tied to what you expect from life and how you want your life to look like.

Before jumping in on the small-business train, a step that many potential owners miss out is establishing their life vision. Although owning a business comes with enormous benefits, it also comes with a price: usually, this amounts to the responsibility that ownership carries.

So, prior to handing in that resignation letter for your day job, try and analyze what is it that's driving you towards dropping it. Here are a few questions that can help you figure out if owning a business is right for you:

- Do you feel that your energy is wasted being a nine-to-fiver?

- Are you having trouble balancing your personal and professional life?

- Do you believe you are missing out by being stuck in an office all day?

- Do you feel unheard/ignored in your day job and would like to have a chance to implement your business ideas and thoughts?

- Would you like to work at your own time, without a strict schedule?

- Would you like to be your own boss and report only to yourself?

- Would you like to be able to take days off whenever you feel like it?

If these thoughts have been bothering you, then your gut instinct is probably right. You should embrace the opportunity and become your own boss.

Why Partner Up with Uber?

There are, however, many (good) reasons why closing your door on the corporate job and starting your own business is a scary, if not crazy, idea. For one, starting your own business will require a lot of learning, patience, and capital that you may not have. Most new business owners need to hold out for a period of time that their business will not be making money, and they need to invest, however little, in advertisement, marketing, branding and the like. And, let's face it, with bills coming in and expenses lining up, the prospect of having to live on very little money and "hope for the best" is not exactly what most of are looking for.

Thankfully, companies such as Uber, offer the best of two worlds. While on the one hand, Uber drivers have all the benefits of being their own bosses, such as choosing their own working hours, having control of how much they earn and not having to report to anyone, they on the other do not need to worry about networking, getting clients and spreading the word about their business.

With the popularity of the service, most drivers can score rides and begin working in a matter of couple of hours from the time they partnered up with Uber. Not only that, but to become a partner it takes only a good driving record, a quick background check and of course, the necessary DMV tests – all of which are basically methods of showing that the person applying is capable of driving.

This, however, is not to say, that you can't establish your own reputation within the Uber pool of drivers. Most people are happy to return to drivers that they like, so if you take good care of being a friendly, reliable Uber driver, you will probably gain a reputation in no time, and have many customers returning. If, at any time, you wish to move out of Uber and begin your own business, this network of clients can definitely come in handy.

Furthermore, if your clients like you, the possibility of earning increases. Since Uber has a rating system for its drivers, doing your best and going out of your way to provide outstanding customer service will benefit you in the long run. Uber drivers with better rating tend to be hired more often, and therefore make more money, which creates an excellent incentive for you to be on your best behavior even on bad days.

Look Before You Leap (The Ins and Outs of Uber)

So – what are the things you need to know before you begin your 'own ride' with Uber? We have covered most of the positive sides – being your own boss, choosing your own hours and passengers, not having to report to anyone – but how does Uber stand when compared to other driving-related professions, and what are the things to look out for when deciding to be an Uber driver?

According to the company's website, Uber drivers surpass all other driving-related careers in terms of income. The only job that comes close in pay is that of a heavy truck driver, but being one tends to take out the benefits that would motivate you to join Uber in the first place. Heavy truck drivers operate under strict schedules, include driving long hours through different states, and generally include having a boss or supervisor. So, if your primary reason why you wanted to join Uber is not the money, but the freedom that it offers you, the prospect of earning similar amounts with heavy truck driving should not interest you.

However, a really important factor to take in when considering becoming an Uber driver is the varying rates and costs of operating in different cities. Uber tailors its prices according to cities, counties and states, so there may be a huge gap between what a San Francisco-based driver earns with that of someone in a less populated, less expensive city.

It is also worth underlining that Uber takes 25% of their drivers' earning to account for their services; on top of that, drivers are in charge of covering their wear-and-tear costs, gas, as well as insurance. So – before you apply for Uber, take a good look at how fuel-efficient your vehicle is, as well as the approximate costs of all the repairs and fixing that may be required due to heavy use. Naturally, if you drive a Jeep Cherokee, you may end up having to pay more than you earn for gas and fixing – which probably will not be the case if you drive a tiny, efficient car.

Finally, the rating system that helps you get rides is not moderated, and the 'people factor' plays a great role. There have been numerous complaints from Uber drivers about bad reviews they got from intoxicated riders who insisted on drinking in the car and, once refused, gave a damaging review to the driver. Just like in any other profession, it pays off to use your common sense and not accept rides from anyone who strikes you as potentially problematic: this may include people refusing to comply with Uber's rules or potentially violent and dangerous customers.

Chapter 4:
How to Build a Successful Business with Uber

Study Your Market

Working with Uber is a business like any other. Just like it doesn't make sense to open an ice-cream parlor in the polar circle, it sometimes doesn't make sense to begin working with Uber in certain areas or cities.

Today's world, however, makes it really easy to do some quality research. As a beginning, you can just go to Google and type in the name of your city followed by "Uber" or "Uber drivers". It should give you a good idea about how popular Uber is in that area, and you will probably run into a couple of drivers' accounts that will help you get started and figure out what the market is.

As a general rule, most drivers (be it Uber or taxi) suggest that hanging around busy spots and figuring out the "peak times" is the best way to maximize your Uber income. If you know your city well, you will have no trouble figuring out where there may be the most tourists, business passengers and general outsiders, who are most likely to use Uber services. It is also an unspoken rule of Uber that late nights, especially on weekends, will bring you plenty of rides.

Once you have as much information as possible, chart out the times that would be most suitable for you to work, and combine them with your desired schedule. You will probably be able to pinpoint when you will make best use of your available time. As an extra, after only a week of driving, Uber provides you with a summary that shows the times when you made the most money, which can always be used for future reference and implemented so that your Uber income is maximized.

Develop a Marketing Plan for Your Business

Like the proverbial tree in the forest, a business is as good as nothing if it is not heard of. Therefore, before beginning to do anything, you need to make sure you get visibility and exposure to your service or business. Otherwise, you might as well sit at the corner and wait for your rides to come, because you will not get further than that.

Although it may appear that marketing with Uber is unnecessary, when making your marketing plan you should focus not on bringing customers to Uber, but bringing customers to you. The plan you come up with should be tailored at promoting yourself *as* an Uber driver, and therefore ensure you that, although your customers will be using the app, they will call you up as their first choice.

Many drivers use the promo coupons given by Uber (usually $10 or $5 off the first ride) and promote them on their social media profiles. If you have a large Twitter following or many friends on Facebook, you can use these channels to let the world know that you are driving for Uber and looking for clients!

With a marketing plan, you can set up some basic goals that you want to achieve, and pinpoint the exact methods how you want to achieve these goals. When you are beginning, marketing can be as easy as asking your friends and family to share your Tweet or Facebook post which offers coupons to new riders.

Set Daily Objects to Get Results Fast

When starting your own business, you should make your daily goal which will help you achieve better status in the long run. By setting a goal you make a norm that you need to fulfill in order to succeed. Having a 'number' that you need to hit each day provides you with enough motivation and a sense of direction which makes it easier to focus on work. And there's no better feeling that ticking off something from your to-do list, right?

Daily objectives mostly revolve around achieving a certain number of clients on a daily basis, which can be some of the people who are your daily clients, as well as new clients. The process of making your daily norm includes a lot of hard work and dedication to your clients, along with a good first impression and communication – which are both big factors in getting return client. By obtaining a certain number of clients you provide more work for yourself and a chance to get better ratings and even more clients, as well as an opportunity to start your own business in which you would be able to be in total control of your work.

When setting daily objectives, it is important not to overestimate your ability to work, and to take into account the market factors. These include the popularity of Uber and Uber rates in a certain area, the time of day and many others.

Ultimately, setting a daily objective enables you to forecast your income for the day, week and month, thus allowing you to be in control of not only how much you earn, but also how much you spend. It allows you to plan for vacations and times off work, as well as make up for any unexpected expenses in your personal life.

Create a Market Even if you're In a Small City

Being an Uber driver in a small city may sound daunting, but actually has many upsides. When you are the big fish in a small pond, you have an opportunity to embrace much more business opportunities than when you are a tiny speck in the sea of Uber drivers.

Most small cities foster relatively tight-knit communities; one of the best ways to market in such small areas is by word of mouth. Spread the word to your friends, neighbors, associates and everyone you know about the convenience of riding with Uber. You may even try to crunch some numbers for them and demonstrate that, for those who own cars but do not use them much, it may be cheaper to ride with Uber due to maintenance costs of their vehicles.

Another great way of profiting with Uber in a small city is through referrals: become an Uber advocate! If you have acquaintances who could benefit from the extra buck, and satisfy all of Uber's conditions, you can refer them and both of you will receive a bonus for it. The only condition future Uber drivers need to fulfill is that they make a set number of rides before the referral bonus is provided. But if people are really interested – that shouldn't be so hard, should it?

All in all, there are no limits to creative ways in which you can market your business or Uber in general; whatever unconventional way of marketing goes through your mind, don't hesitate to try it. It will probably cost you nothing, but it can always turn out to be a great idea!

Chapter 5:
How to Promote Your Uber Business

The Importance of Branding

The most common thing associated with branding is a company's logo; yet a brand signifies much more than a piece of design. A brand represents everything a business (or individual) stands for, including their values, ideas and vision. A brand is reflected in everything from how e-mails are written to what the offices look and feel like. In short – a brand is the complete customer experience provided by a business.

When explained like this, it is a no brainer why branding represents such an important factor for all things business: it is one of the most important factors determining the relationship between the business and the client, and it plays a deciding role in attraction of new customers, retaining of old customers and overall business growth.

So, what are the basics of branding?

It all begins with a message: a message that you want to send out to your clients and anyone who gets in touch with your brand. As an Uber partner, or an owner of a transportation business, you need to figure out what your message is. You may target business clients – and therefore send a message of being an Uber partner that takes meetings seriously, is always on time and manages to get you from Point A to Point B without delay or hassle. If you are targeting younger people, you probably want to send the message of being fun, communicative and easy-going (say, you won't mind waiting for a couple of minutes while the group is gathered, or you won't have a problem making a couple of stops on the way home).

If you work hard at establishing your brand, one of the primary benefits is **recognition**. Although as an Uber partner you cannot really go out of your way with visual branding, there is still a way, mainly through your interaction with riders, that you set yourself apart and make their ride memorable enough that they will remember you the next time they need a lift.

When your clients recognize you, they can **trust you** and also **know what to expect**. In that way, you are ensuring that, before they request your service, they will know not only what's allowed, but also what isn't. It will help you maintain a steady client base and avoid uncomfortable situations; on the other hand, it will also ensure that your clients return, knowing what benefits using your services brings to them.

This kind of consistency also helps **you stay on track**. Knowing that your customers are expecting a certain type of service, be it the way you are dressed or the way you communicate with them, will always keep you in check and ensure that you do your best during business hours. It will help you stay focused and motivate you to always come up with new ways of demonstrating the core of your business values to prospective, new and returning clients.

Designing Your Own Website

With the importance of marketing, having your own website as a way for promoting your services is an important first step. Today, not having a website usually sends a message of unreliability and suspiciousness, which is not the way to attract clients.

Luckily, the popularity of the Internet has made it easier than ever to create your own website without having to call in designers and shell out a lot of money for it. There are plenty of online services offering full interactive website designs at low costs, and hosting is cheaper than ever!

Your website should include some basic information about your business, and, naturally, be consistent with the brand message that your business wants to send. Once again –

websites tailored for business professionals will look much more different than those aimed at attracting young party-goers.

The design of your website is like your online office, which is why you need to take time and figure out how you want the website to look – that is, what kind of an impression do you want to make on the site's visitors.

On top of that, websites need to be regularly updated in order to serve their purpose. If what your website is saying appears to be outdated, its visitors will probably dismiss your business as shady and move on to a company that seems more up-to-date and trendy.

What's really important to keep in mind, and what many small business owners tend to forget, is that your website is just a part of the entire package you are offering. Focusing on building an amazing website, yet failing to deliver in terms of your services or client experience will likely have a negative impact in the long run. Make sure that your website is great, but also keep in mind that clients seeing a great website will also expect other features, which you mustn't miss out on.

Build Your Business with Business Cards

We all know that the Internet is a huge market, allowing us to send our message to a large audience and reach a large population with our marketing. But, good old traditional networking via word of mouth and business cards should not be underestimated. Albeit smaller in reach, this method of marketing allows you to have a face-to-face interaction with your client, and ensure that they become your regular. When a client is satisfied with the services provided, you can make best of the situation, hand out your business card, and expect that they will be returning soon.

Business cards are a great way of doing marketing while doing your job – as you complete a ride with your customer, and you exchange pleasantries, you can hand him your business card (or even a few) that they can refer to when they wish to call you again. In order to incentivize the client to take up the card, you may come up with a promotional offer – such as 10% off on the first ride to whoever brings your card.

Do not be fooled with the traditional character of this method: many individuals, both young and old, still feel the impact of being handed a business card, and sometimes, this can be a game-changer when it comes to ensuring a returning client.

It now goes without saying that, like your website, your business card should be in line with the message your brand is trying to send. An inconsistent message is worse than no message at all, so make sure that you keep in mind the principal values of your message, and implement them into your business card design.

Once you have your business cards printed, have them on you at all times – networking should not only be reserved for the time you spend driving. Who knows? You may run into an old acquaintance at the supermarket that complains of unreliable taxi service and is looking for an alternative, or strike up a conversation with a stranger who can no longer drive and is looking for a solution to his problems. Hand out your business card to whomever may be interested in your services; you never know who may give you a ring.

Dominate With Video Marketing

A relatively new medium for promoting your brand, video marketing may just give you an edge over the competition that you have been looking for. Unlike the previous few, this one may require slightly more work, but its unconventional and unique nature is sure to attract attention and score some customers.

Think about this: between 2013 and 2014, there has been a 43% increase in the amount of videos watched online. That means that 38.2 billion videos were watched within a one-year period. And, though nobody is sure where this is going to end up, one thing is certain: more and more videos are being watched every day, and video marketing is the way to go in the future.

While your opportunities may seem limited as a mere Uber partner – there are still things you can do to promote your business and services using video. For instance, you can ask your clients for a video testimonial about how they felt about the ride and then upload it to Snapchat or your social media profiles and website. Alternatively, you can collect a number of testimonials, combine them in a single video, and use it as promotional material for your business.

Relationship Building Is KING

The most important message, therefore, that you can take from this Chapter on building your brand is that in order to grow successfully (and sustainably!) what you need to do is foster a trusting, caring relationship with your clients, which will ensure that they will always come back to you for all their transportation needs and be happy to refer you whenever they have the chance!

Relationship building operates on many levels, all of which are equally important and need to be taken into account: beginning with how you interact with each of your riders during their Uber trip, through being a reliable and dependable Uber partner, all the way to mass means of communication such as your website, social media and business card.

Without your clients feeling loved, appreciated and honored in their interaction with you, you cannot expect to go farther than being a random ride someone gets on Uber; and as such, you cannot expect to make a decent living out of partnering up with Uber for your transportation services. So – take advantage of the huge client base offered by Uber, and use it to create your own world of loyal customers that will keep coming back.

An important piece of advice shared by many experts when it comes to building and sustaining a relationship with your client base is to remember that they, too, are people. Too many small business owners get caught up in having to score and having to expand their client base that they forget all of their clients have their own specific needs and likes, and that a small gesture of appreciation (even remembering someone's name) can go a long way in ensuring that you are respected and admired for what you do.

Just like local shop-owners who always knew everyone's name in the neighborhood and gave candy and sweets to children, you too can make sure, through being respectful and caring in your relationship with each client, that you are always remembered for the quality of service provided and returned to.

This, in itself, is a lesson for whatever business venture you may be interested in, and is not limited to being an Uber partner. However, remember Uber reviews and ratings? This is where relationship-building are translated into numbers. Satisfied clients with whom you have managed to establish, at worst, a friendly connection, will always be happy to write raving reviews. And when you have amazing reviews on Uber, you will always be in on the best rides, and the next opportunity to make money will be right around the corner – literally!

Chapter 6:
Meet Big Rob "The Uber Driver"

Who Is Big Rob?

Just to give you a glimpse of who I am, I just your average "country boy" from North Carolina with big dreams. I grew up in a single parent household and in the inner city. I didn't grow up with a lot of money and faced many setbacks and hardships along the way. With those things going on in my life didn't stop me for achieving any type of success in life. I've always was a man of great vision and determination to make it in this life. All I needed was these three things. Those three things is *THE SKILL, THE MINDSET,* and *THE OPPORTUNIY* or vehicle to get me towards my destination of financial success.

Why I Decided To Join Uber?

I decided to drive for Uber because I was looking for the same thing that most people want, which was financial freedom. I've tried many different home based businesses in the past which all have been nothing but total failures. At one point in my journey in the home business arena, I've gotten to the point to just give up mainly because all you see on the internet is a bunch of hype, and no integrity if any. It's very hard to find a great home based business opportunity that truly works for anyone as well as a mentor that will show you how to make money. I found an ad online that was advertising *"Get Paid to Drive."* That intrigued me to find out more about it. Once I saw what it was and how simple it was, I just signed up. Keep in mind that I didn't do much with it at first. What motivated me to actually take action on it was a post from a friend of mines on Facebook. I saw a post on Facebook where I see him make $900 bucks with Uber. Once I saw this, I immediately said to myself, "I gotta give this a try." I started doing Uber around late November, but things were slow at that point and only made around $70 bucks per week which wasn't too bad. Right around the first of the year, I really saw my Uber business pick up dramatically. I was averaging around $200-$300 starting off, then it really start going into high-gear afterwards. Here is proof of what I was making.

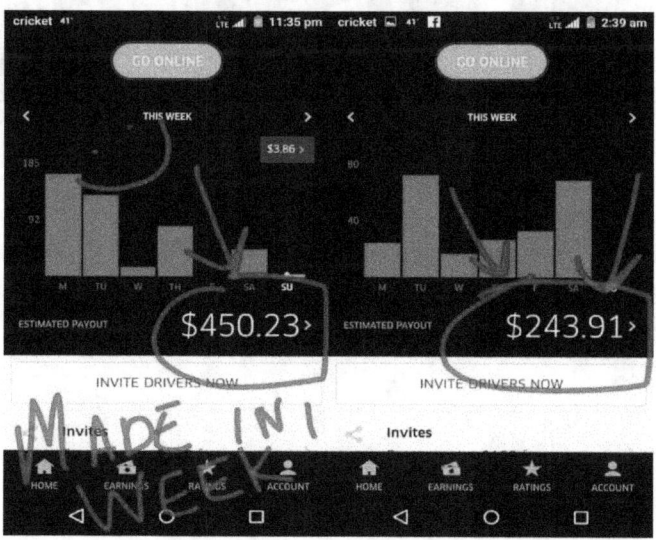

After making this type of money only putting in on average 20+ hours a week, I said to myself, *"This definitely can turn into a full-time income opportunity for me."*

My Experience with Uber

Being an Uber driver does has its ups and downs, but overall I must say I love Uber. I like the flexibly that Uber offers. For instance, you get to choose your own hours. You decide when you want to turn the mobile app on or off. You call all the shots. You can earn as much as you truly want. There is really no limit on how much money you can make with Uber. I love meeting new people and building lasting relationships. To me, it's not just about picking up riders and making money. It's more about giving your riders an experience that they will never forget. I had people say to me, "I'm a very cool Uber driver." I just love to connect with people. Plus you get to travel to different parts of the city and state. For instance, I had the privilege to go to Charlotte, North Carolina to the NFL Playoffs to see the Carolina Panthers and Seahawks play just with Uber. I had to take people to the stadium and drop them off to their destinations. I met some really great people there and most of them wanted me to come back to Charlotte, NC.

I can say that Uber is a great opportunity for those looking for change. If you love meeting new people, travel, and make money then you definitely need to partner up with Uber today.

IMAGINE TOTAL FINANCIAL FREEDOM

If You're Ready To Start Making Some Serious Money With Uber, then go to my site to sign up

www.ubertoday.info